HELLO

BLACK

MAN

Dedication Page

TO MY FATHER
Herbert Charles Gustavis

To know you, is to love you. Through your mental sharpness and your wisdom, I have developed quite a personality of my own. I've never questioned our relationship or the bond that we managed to develop. I may not always tell you, but know that I appreciate you. You have inspired me in many ways and for that reason, I dedicate this first edition of "HELLO BLACK MAN" to you. Thank you for the stories and the laughs that we have shared over the years. I pray this journal can help build and grow our relationship to new heights.

TO MY SON
Landon Ahmad Jenkins (Lando Legend)

So often I feel that I fall short of being the father you need me to be. You are wise beyond your years and filled with such passion, charisma and vigor for life. You seek answers to many questions that I often times have no response. Everyday I'm seeking to find ways to draw you to me and fill any voids that I have failed to recognize. To you son, I dedicate this first edition of "HELLO BLACK MAN". Together we will expound on getting to know one another through this journal and the many more to come. Dad loves you Landon and you will always be great in my eyes.

Hello Black Man

A GUIDED JOURNAL EXPERIENCE

This guided journal is being made available to build character, confidence and define the inner person.

It has been deemed clear that our culture and our past has hindered black men from being open and vulnerable.

For centuries our male ancestors have built impenetrable walls. Communication has forever been obsolete. The inability to express oneself has lead to internal suffrage and problematic progression. Hello Black Man is geared toward bridging the gap and burning emotional barriers through written communication.

As a black man, I have spent my entire life being ridiculed for what has been identified as a lack of emotional intelligence. I was raised to believe that a man who displays emotions or bares his weakness is viewed as defenseless.

With this journal, I'm seeking to change the narrative and create a space for men to be who they are in a judgement free zone. Let's successfully unwrap insecurities and build positive, lifelong connections through open channels of communications.

Thank you for your support and I hope that this helps you in the same way it has helped me!

These are the stories, thoughts,
feelings and beliefs of

———————————————,

an amazing black man!

This is as plain as I can put it...

If you get caught up in the things over which you
have no control, it will adversely affect those
things over which you have control.

Date:

1. Hello Black Man, what is your most impactful childhood memory and how did it change you?

This is as plain as I can put it...

Your capabilities will soon meet your opportunities.
Will you be ready?

Date:

2. Hello Black Man, talk about your biggest fears in life.

This is as plain as I can put it....

If you are truly a good person,
Stop trying to figure out why someone doesn't like you.
They don't even like themselves.

Date:

3. Hello Black Man, explain your relationship with your mother or a mother figure and how it has helped shaped you.

This is as plain as I can put it...

Sometimes the extra mile is the mile you need
to get where you are going.

Date:
_____

_____

_____

_____

_____

_____

_____

_____

_____

_____

_____

_____

_____

_____

_____

_____

_____

_____

4. Hello Black Man, explain your relationship with your father or a father figure and how it has helped shaped you.

This is as plain as I can put it...

Be careful...
Some people look to be opportunistic vs seeking opportunity.

Date:

5. Hello Black Man, what did you and your friends do for fun when you were in high school? Talk about your most memorable high school experience.

_____

_____

_____

_____

_____

_____

_____

_____

_____

_____

_____

_____

_____

_____

_____

_____

_____

_____

_____

_____

This is as plain as I can put it...

From time to time you are going to help people
that can't, won't, don't help you. That's ok.
But use all diligence about helping people who won't help themselves
.

Date: _____

_____

_____

_____

_____

_____

_____

_____

_____

_____

_____

_____

_____

_____

_____

_____

_____

6. Hello Black Man, talk about where you grew up. Describe your house, your neighbors, the environment.

This is as plain as I can put it...

Hang in there. You are on the right path. Press your way.

Date: _____

7. Hello Black Man, how do you think others describe you? How do you describe yourself?

This is as plain as I can put it...

You can't make someone appreciate you. Stop trying.
You can make yourself absent. Get moving.

Date:

8. Hello Black Man, thinking back on life, what do you feel was your biggest mistake and what do you think you learned from it?

This is as plain as I can put it...

Hear people LOUD & CLEAR.....when they say nothing.

.

Date: _____

_____
_____
_____
_____
_____
_____
_____
_____
_____
_____
_____
_____
_____
_____
_____
_____
_____
_____
_____
_____

9. Hello Black Man, describe the effectiveness of your communication skills.

This is as plain as I can put it...

You can NOT impress someone ...
who constantly wants to be impressed.

Date:

10. Hello Black Man, describe your religious beliefs or preferences. What does faith and spirituality mean to you?

This is as plain as I can put it...

Stop talking about it, thinking about it, wondering about it,
posting about it, complaining about it,
PUT THE WORK IN.

Date:

11. Hello Black Man, what's your idea of a perfect relationship? If you could build a mate what all qualities would they possess?

This is as plain as I can put it...

In certain circumstances...
to show someone the value of your skills & talents...
Take them away.

Date:

12. Hello Black Man, what's your dream job and what can you do to make this dream a reality.

This is as plain as I can put it...

I've never seen a LEADER that didn't LISTEN.

Date: _____

.
_____

_____

_____

_____

_____

_____

_____

_____

_____

_____

_____

_____

_____

_____

_____

_____

_____

_____

13. Hello Black Man, what are some goals that you have accomplished? Talk about goals you wish to accomplish and write a plan as to how you will accomplish them.

This is as plain as I can put it...

Someone gave up on you. They made a mistake.

Date:

14. Hello Black Man, talk about your taste in music. What genres do you prefer? What are your top 5 songs of all times?

This is as plain as I can put it...

Every plug needs a source. Be the source.

Date:

15. Hello Black Man, discuss your credit score? Talk about maintaining a good credit score and what you are currently doing to monitor and improve your scores.

This is as plain as I can put it...

You don't need to work through every problem;
Sometimes, just work around it.

Date:

16. Hello Black Man, did you attend college? Why or why not? If so, what was your major and how did your college experience shape you?

_____

_____

_____

_____

_____

_____

_____

_____

_____

_____

_____

_____

_____

_____

_____

_____

_____

_____

This is as plain as I can put it...

Be the hunter or be hunted.

Date: _____

.

17. Hello Black Man, what does being black mean to you? Name some advantages and disadvantages.

This is as plain as I can put it...

While trying to be great, ensure that you are grateful.

Date:

18. Hello Black Man, talk about your past relationships? What are breaking points for you? Describe your love language.

This is as plain as I can put it...

Listen to their words, but notice their actions.

Date:

19. Hello Black Man, describe your most embarrassing moment in life.

This is as plain as I can put it...

No one's life is as they expected it to be.

Date: _____

_____

_____

_____

_____

_____

_____

_____

_____

_____

_____

_____

_____

_____

_____

_____

_____

_____

20. Hello Black Man, what is an idea marriage from your point of view?
Describe what you think makes marriage work.

This is as plain as I can put it...

Eliminating noise, gives you better vision.

Date:

21. Hello Black Man, talk about things you are great at and your known talents. What are your hidden talents that only you or very few know about?

This is as plain as I can put it...

Don't waste today...you will never get it back.

Date: _____

22. Hello Black Man, what qualities make you a strong person? What traits of your character do you feel need improvement?

This is as plain as I can put it...

Pay it forward today even if only just a little...
someone really needs it.

Date:

23. Hello Black Man, describe your relationship with your friends. What makes you a good friend? Who is your best friend?

This is as plain as I can put it...

Today speak with your actions.

Date: _____

24. Hello Black Man, what or who motivates you? Describe how it feels to be motivated.

This is as plain as I can put it...

Hang in there. You are on the right path. Press your way.

Date: _____

_____

_____

_____

_____

_____

_____

_____

_____

_____

_____

_____

_____

_____

_____

_____

_____

_____

25. Hello Black Man, what is one thing you wish you could change about yourself? Describe steps to change.

This is as plain as I can put it...

Always invest in yourself and demand returns.

Date:

26. Hello Black Man, do you have any bad habits? What methods have you tried to break them?

This is as plain as I can put it...

You are not meant for everyone.

Date:

27. Hello Black Man, contact someone you hadn't heard from in a while. Write down how the conversation went. Explain how it felt to reconnect or to pick up from where you left off.

This is as plain as I can put it...

Focus on improving not impressing.

Date:

28. Hello Black Man, what's the hardest decision you've ever made? Was it beneficial? Were you happy with the decision you made?

This is as plain as I can put it...

If you let up for one second,
that's where you will finish...SECOND.

Date:
_____

.

29. Hello Black Man, are you a risk taker? What's the most dangerous thing you've ever done? How did you feel afterwards?

This is as plain as I can put it...

If you regret yesterday on today,
then not one day but two days are wasted...
Each day, hour, minute, second is a fresh start.

Date:

30. Hello Black Man, write a letter to your younger self.

This is as plain as I can put it...

If you're not willing to risk it all by betting on yourself...
why would anyone else?

Date: _____

31. Hello Black Man, what's the most uncharacteristic thing you've ever done to impress someone? Were they impressed? Explain what you feel you would have done differently.

_____

_____

_____

_____

_____

_____

_____

_____

_____

_____

_____

_____

_____

_____

_____

_____

_____

_____

_____

This is as plain as I can put it...

Take care of your character when you "think" nobody is looking,
somebody is watching.

Date:

32. Hello Black Man, can you explain how your parents showed you love, and how they showed love to one another, or where you first learned what love looked like?

This is as plain as I can put it...

When you truly believe in yourself,
it really doesn't matter what others think!

Date:

33. Hello Black Man, discuss your financial goals. Describe your idea of financial stability.

This is as plain as I can put it...

Keep your vision clear...
because if your vision becomes blurred,
the target is hard to find.

Date:

34. Hello Black Man, are you physically fit? What are your fitness goals? Have you had a physical? If not, schedule one and write down the results?

_____

_____

_____

_____

_____

_____

_____

_____

_____

_____

_____

_____

_____

_____

_____

_____

_____

_____

This is as plain as I can put it...

The best things in life aren't..things at all.

Date:

35. Hello Black Man, tell me about a time when you allowed your anger to overcome you. How were you able to calm yourself? What did it feel like after the fact?

This is as plain as I can put it...

Progress always involve risks.
You cant steal second base with your foot on first.

Date: _____

36. Hello Black Man, what principles and values would you instill in your children? How do they differ from or align with the ones what were instilled in you as a child?

This is as plain as I can put it...

having good things is ok...going good places is even better...
but when you are around good people...
the first two things don't matter.

Date:

37. Hello Black Man, explain in detail any trust issues or insecurities you may battle.

This is as plain as I can put it...

be intentional in finding out ways to bring out
the best in those that surround you on a regular basis.

Date:

38. Hello Black Man, explain how you handle stress or things that really frustrate you. What are your coping mechanisms?

This is as plain as I can put it...

Be more concerned with your character than your reputation.
Character is what your really are.
Reputation is just what people say you are.

Date:

39. Hello Black Man, describe your current relationship with your family. Who do you turn to for advice? What about that person makes you feel as if your information is secure?

This is as plain as I can put it...

Be more concerned with your character than your reputation.
Character is what your really are.
Reputation is just what people say you are.

Date: _____

.

40. Hello Black Man, talk about the things and ways you like to be appreciated.

This is as plain as I can put it...

Think deeply, speak gently, love much, work hard,
give freely, be kind, and leave the rest to God.

Date:

41. Hello Black Man, describe in detail, your most memorable dream.

This is as plain as I can put it...

Talent is God-given, be humble; fame is man given, be thankful; conceit is self-given, be careful.

Date:

42. Hello Black Man, how would you describe your mental health? Would you ever seek professional help, like counseling or therapy? Why or why not?

This is as plain as I can put it...

Your goal:
To be better today than you were yesterday;
to be better tomorrow than you are today.

Date: _____

43. Hello Black Man, do you own a business? Discuss any business plans or ideas. What steps would you like to take to start your own business or improve your current business?

_____

_____

_____

_____

_____

_____

_____

_____

_____

_____

_____

_____

_____

_____

_____

_____

_____

_____

_____

This is as plain as I can put it...

TAKE the opportunity, don't wait for it to be given.

Date: _____

44. Hello Black Man, what type of movies do you enjoy? Discuss your favorite movie. What do you like most about it? List your top 5 movies. What makes these movies great?

This is as plain as I can put it...

When you want to succeed as bad as you want to breath...
then you will be successful.

Date: _____

.

_____

_____

_____

_____

_____

_____

_____

_____

_____

_____

_____

_____

_____

_____

_____

_____

_____

_____

45. Hello Black Man, explain your political views. Would you ever run for a political office? If so, which office? If not, why?

This is as plain as I can put it...

The job of a great leader is not to have many followers,
but to train many leaders.

Date:

46. Hello Black Man, talk about your most memorable travels. From departure to return. Highlight the highs and the lows. What's your bucket list of places to visit?

This is as plain as I can put it...

Visualize greatness...
you move toward what you see everyday.

Date:

47. Hello Black Man, you've won the lottery, $100M, describe your plans.

This is as plain as I can put it...

You never get ahead of anyone,
as long as you try to get even with them.

Date: _____

48. Hello Black Man, does anyone in your family have health issues? How has it affected you or the ones to whom they are directly connected?

This is as plain as I can put it...

You don't need a dream...you need a goal...
you don't need hope...you need hard work...#nodaysoff.

Date: _____

49. Hello Black Man, explain ways in which you believe love can be kept alive in relationships.

This is as plain as I can put it...

You are better off with honest enemies than fake friends.

Date:

50. Hello Black Man, describe your dream house? Attach or draw a floor plan.

This is as plain as I can put it...

As you intermingle today,
remember everyone is going through something
that you know absolutely nothing about. BE NICE!

Date:

51. Hello Black Man, explain your most significant loss. How has it changed you as a person?

This is as plain as I can put it...

Invest in yourself when no one will.
Dont be your biggest doubter!

Date:

52. Hello Black Man, describe in detail what happy looks like and feels like to you.

A GLIMPSE OF
THE AUTHOR

Jamey Jenkins is a native of Hazlehurst,MS by way of It,MS(yes there is a place known as It, Mississippi). He is the son of Jerone Durr and Herbert Gustavis. He is the proud father of three amazing children, Ajah, Jamyn and Landon.

Jamey Jenkins is a graduate of Alcorn State University with a degree in Political Science. While attending Alcorn State he became well known for dominating the basketball scene in intramural basketball at the old gym. His jumper is still the coldest, even in his 40s. He is in fact planning to try out for the New York Knicks next season. He currently holds an undefeated record in spades. He recently won the city-wide spades tournament beating out the mayor and all in attendance. (Ask anybody. These are facts).

Jamey has been a member of Kappa Alpha Psi fraternity since Spring 2000. He boasts the smoothest shimmy in the entire organization (so says the ladies). Since his departure from Alcorn State he has been climbing the ranks of Nissan North American. Jamey is the owner and CEO of a photography company, Big Pretty Pictures. Jamey has recently began his journey into helping mentor and grow small businesses through his strategic marketing company, JameyJenkinsInc. He is a philanthropist, who strongly believes and adheres to the principle of "never forgetting from where you came ."

Jamey debuts his first guided journal of the series Hello Black Man with hopes of expanding the brand and reaching his brethren globally.

If you want to know more about the movement, please visit the website at http://www.helloblackman.com,
where you can review the book and check out Hello Black Man official apparel.

DIE WITH NO "GREAT IDEAS"

Made in the USA
Coppell, TX
26 January 2024

28213071R10066